THE CROSS KIRK PEEBLES

by

STEVE DUBÉ

This story of the Cross Kirk
is dedicated with love
to my grand-daughter Laura

First published 2016
Kirklands Press
16 Kirkland Street
Peebles
EH45 8EU
© Steve Dubé

ISBN 978-0-9956703-03

Printed in Peebles by Elmbank Print,
8 Elcho Street Brae, Peebles EH45 8HU

CONTENTS

Introduction

This small book is intended to encourage visitors and residents of Peebles to learn about, explore and interpret the ruins of one of the oldest and most important medieval buildings of the town.

I am conscious that I walk in distinguished footsteps. Dr Clement Bryce Gunn was instrumental in securing for future generations what was in his day a neglected Cross Kirk site. He also researched and produced a remarkable series of volumes on the historic churches in and around Peebles. He in turn often paid fulsome tribute to the work of Robert Renwick for his histories of Peebles and his work on the Burgh records. Both these antiquarians have informed this book, along with James Walter Buchan and William Chambers in their histories of the town and former county of Peeblesshire. I recommend their work to anyone interested in the history of the Cross Kirk and this lovely border town.

I'm grateful for the help, advice and encouragement freely given by Ruth Noble and Ronald Ireland and by Rosemary Hannay and Chris Sawers at the Tweeddale Museum. Thanks also to Emma Scott for her photo of the 2016 Beltane service. Ian McLeod and Ruth Lowe at Elmbank Print were always helpful and professional. Thanks to the Tweeddale Society for their support. And my wife Janet was patient and a careful proof reader.

THE CROSS KIRK
An Outline

The ruins of the Cross Kirk occupy a quiet, sheltered site a short, well-signposted walk from the town centre of Peebles. This was once the focus of one of the three most popular medieval pilgrimages in Scotland.

The Cross Kirk was founded in 1261 by order of King Alexander III, following the discovery of a *"magnificent and venerable cross"* near a grave containing the dismembered skeleton of a man.[1]

People quickly came to the conclusion that the bones were the remains of an early Christian bishop called Nicholas who had been martyred by the Romans, and the church incorporated a purpose-built shrine to the martyr.

Statue of Alexander III above west door, St Giles, Edinburgh

The kirk was given over to the care of a lesser-known religious order known as the Trinitarians. It rapidly became a focus of pilgrimage and some 300 years later became a Trinitarian convent or friary, the only

---

[1] Royal Commission on the Ancient and Historical Monuments of Scotland (RCAHMS), *An Inventory of the Ancient Monuments of Peeblesshire, Vol II*, 1967, pp203-204

monastic settlement in the former county of Peeblesshire. Before long people came to believe that the relics enshrined within its walls included a piece of the cross on which Jesus was crucified.

The church and monastery were described by Dr William Dalgleish in the early 18th century as having been *"the principal church on the Tweed westward, after the magnificent abbey of Melrose, and the only one of the conventual kind"*.[2]

Like all medieval friaries it had the full range of monastic buildings such as a cloister and chapter house. There was a dovecote in the grounds. Unlike monks, who lived secluded lives, friars like these were active in the community, ministering to people in the locality and further afield. It's not known how many lived at the Cross Kirk. The historian William Chambers mentions 70, a figure repeated by Gunn[3] though neither names the source. By the time the Reformation reached Peebles in 1560 there were only five.

Until the Reformation the friars were often joined by devotees offering prayers for the salvation of their souls or relief from sickness and disease. And there were huge gatherings on

---

[2] Letter from Dr William Dalgleish, Minister at Peebles, to George Henry Hutton, quoted in Robert Renwick, *A Peebles Aisle and Monastery,* Glasgow: Carson & Nicol, 1897, p48 n2

[3] Clement Bryce Gunn, *The Three Priests of Peebles,* James Lewis, Selkirk, 1894, p13

special feast days, particularly the town's historic Beltane festival every May.[4]

The festival was abandoned at the Reformation but revived in 1897 and since 1930 it has included a religious service that again attracts hundreds of people the Cross Kirk at the start of a series of events over eight or nine days. And throughout the year it draws curious visitors and local people of all ages who use the grounds for recreation

THE LEGEND

Seal of Alexander

The story begins during the reign of Alexander III (1249-1286).

"On the 9th of May, 1261, in the thirteenth year of King Alexander, a stately and venerable cross was found at Peebles, in the presence of good men, priests, clerics and burgesses. But it is quite unknown in what year and by what persons it was hidden there."[5]

These are the words of the Scottish chronicler John of Fordun, said to have been written (in Latin) at some time between the years 1384 and 1387.

They come from a text called the Scotichronicon. This is a chronicle of Scottish history compiled by Walter Bower (1385-

---

[4] This event now takes place in June

[5] Clement Bryce Gunn, *The Church and Monastery of the Holy Cross of Peebles*, James Lewis, Selkirk, 1909, p1

1449), abbot of Inchcolm Abbey, now a romantic ruin on an island in the Firth of Forth, near Edinburgh.

The chronicle, written between 1447 and 1449, says people believed the cross was hidden by Christians around the year 296 when they were being persecuted during the reign of the Roman Emperor Maximian. The chronicle continues: *"Not long after this a stone urn was discovered there, about three or four paces from the spot where that glorious cross had been found. It contained the ashes and bones of a man's body – torn limb from limb, as it were. Whose relics these are no one knows as yet. Some, however, think they are the relics of him whose name was found written on the very stone wherein that holy cross was lying. Now there was carved on that stone,*

A page from the Scotichronicon shows a Gaelic poet praising Alexander III at his coronation in 1249

outside: **Locus Sancti Nicholai Episcopi** (the Tomb of the Bishop Saint Nicholas). *Moreover, in the very spot where the cross was found, many a miracle was and is wrought by that cross; and the people poured and still pour thither in crowds, devoutly bringing their offerings and vows to God. Wherefore the King, by the advice of the Bishop of Glasgow, had a* *handsome church made there, to the honour of God and the Holy Cross."[6]*

The story of the cross, the stone and the urn emerged in an age when all sorts of relics were suddenly discovered across Britain by "good men, priests, clerics and burgesses". Perhaps the most famous is the "grave" of King Arthur at Glastonbury. Peebles was in the diocese of Glasgow so the bishop may well have liked the idea of a new shrine in his patch. And the town was conveniently located on the pilgrimage route from Glasgow to the Cistercian abbey of Melrose with its shrine of St Waltheof. The abbey's shrine to its saintly second abbot was built in 1240, just two decades before the miraculous discoveries at Peebles. The Cross Kirk would later become linked to the "Holy Cross" itself, joining a very long list of religious places claiming possession of a piece of the wood used to crucify Jesus.

One or two elements of the original story don't quite fit, although we shouldn't blame Fordun for that. He wrote more than 100 years after the event and probably got his information from monks like himself. And anyway, this section of his chronicle was compiled, as we have seen, by Walter Bower of Inchcolm Abbey, in the mid-15th century. Bower added to and embellished Fordun's notes and has been described as less competent than Fordun - *"garrulous, irrelevant and inaccurate",* and someone who *"makes every important occurrence an excuse for a long-winded moral*

---

[6] Ibid

discourse".[7] The text passed through even more hands before it was first published in the *Scotichronicon* in 1722.

SAINT NICHOLAS

So who was Saint Nicholas? At this distance we can't know how much of the tale is true, embroidered or even invented. But we do know that it doesn't entirely add up. For instance, it's unclear why the year 296 was chosen so precisely. Maximian wasn't even in Britain that year and was not at that time connected at all with the often-changing chain of command that governed the province of Britannia.[8] The "great persecution" set in train by Maximian's co-emperor Diocletian began in 290 but it only reached Britain in the year 300. Its consequences were severe. Among more than ten thousand victims were six bishops, including Nicholas, Bishop of Penrhyn (Glasgow). Peebles was in the diocese of Glasgow, so it is entirely possible that he was killed at this location, or that, for some reason, his body was brought here for burial. Maybe he actually came from Peebles?

Fordun carefully avoids making any claims for the identity of the bones found by those good men, priests, clerics and burgesses. But the 17th century historian Thomas Dempster seems to know more.

---

[7] A.W. Ward & A. R. Waller, *The Cambridge History of English and American Literature Vol 2*, New York, 2000, quoted at Bartleby.com

[8] Peter Salway, *Roman Britain*, Clarendon Press, 1981, p205 et al

He repeats Fordun's story about the Maximian persecution, but goes on to describe the remains as those of a Culdee – an early British Christian strongly influenced by Druidic beliefs - who was one of the first bishops of the Church of Scotland.[9]

Nicholas, Bishop of Penrhyn was indeed a Culdee and a number of historians have recorded that this was one of the Church's early martyrs.[10]

But this otherwise unknown bishop has a very much better known rival. Some modern historians believe that the best candidate for the saint named on the now-lost stone may possibly be St Nikolaos or Nicholas, the 4th-century Bishop of Myra, in Asia Minor - today the town of Demre on the Mediterranean coast of Turkey.[11]

St Nikolaos of Myra

---

[9] Thomas Dempster, *The Ecclesiastical History of the Scottish People*, published in 1627

[10] AW Haddon & W Stubbs, *Councils and ecclesiastical documents relating to Great Britain and Ireland*, Clarendon Press 1869, Vol. I, p32. Thomas Fuller, *Church. History of Britain*, University Press, Oxford, 1845, Vol. I, p20.

[11] RCAHMS, Op Cit Vol 2, p204

The patron saint of sailors, he was said to have performed so many miracles that he was known as Nikolaos the Wonderworker. But his greater claim to fame resulted from his habit of secretly giving gifts. Over the years this created the myth of Santa Claus. Accordingly, Peebles has a claim to being the burial place of the first Father Christmas!

No-one knows how his bones might have got to Peebles, and there are rival claims to be the site of Santa's grave. These would in time become much travelled bones, but they first rested in his home town. By the 11th century pilgrims journeyed in droves to the saint's grave in Myra and reported countless miracles.

The tomb of St Nicholas in the ruined Byzantine church at Demre, Myra

These were said to be obtained by using a clear watery liquid smelling like rose water that appeared to seep from the grave every year. Pilgrims called it *manna* or *myrrh*.

Reverence for the saint spread throughout the Christian world. The first, 6th century, church was extended and by the 11th century there was a monastery on the site, with a community of monks looking after the shrine and catering for the crowds of pilgrims.

Soon afterwards, Myra was overcome by invaders from the Islamic world. At first the impact was negligible.

But mounting conflict between Christians and Muslims led to concerns that access to the tomb might become difficult - with both religious and commercial consequences. The Italian cities of Venice along with Bari competed to become the new home for the relics. And in 1087, in spite of objections from monks at the shrine, sailors from Bari seized some of the

Pilgrims at the shrine of St Nicholas in Bari, painted by Gentile da Fabriano in 1425

bones. They took them to Bari, where there are now two churches at his shrine - one Roman Catholic and one Orthodox.[12]

According to tradition, the rest of the bones were collected by Venetian sailors during the first crusade and taken to Venice, where there is now a church to St. Nicholas. The tradition was given some credence by scientific analysis of the relics in Bari and Venice, which showed that they came from the same skeleton.

The magic liquid continues to be produced from the relics in Bari. Vials of *myrrh* have been taken all over the world for centuries, and can still be obtained in Bari, where a flask is extracted from the tomb every year on 6 December, the saint's feast day. As Bari is a harbour and the tomb is below

---

[12] www.en.wikipedia.org/wiki/Saint_Nicholas

sea level, sceptics suggest that the liquid is nothing more than sea water produced by capillary action.

In 2009 the Turkish Government announced that it would formally ask the Italian government to return the bones to Turkey as they had been illegally removed from his homeland. Or had they? In 1993, a grave was found on the small Turkish island of Gemile, east of Rhodes, which historians asserted was the real tomb of Saint Nicholas. And an Irish tradition states that the relics of Saint Nicholas were stolen from Myra by Norman crusaders in the 12th century and buried near Thomastown, County Kilkenny, where a stone slab marks the site of his grave.[13]

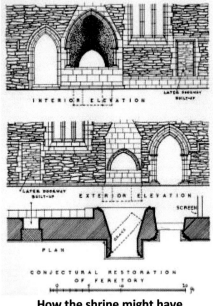

How the shrine might have looked © Historic Environment Scotland

The Cross Kirk shrine was destroyed at the Reformation and no trace of it remains,

---

[13] Ibid

THE FACTS[14]

The year 1261 is given by John of Fordun as the foundation date for the Cross Kirk. It was designed around a shrine in the south wall on the spot where the urn was found and was ministered by members of the Order of the Most Holy Trinity and the Redemption of Captives, the Trinitarian or Red Friars.

All Trinitarian churches – there were 11 in Scotland - were dedicated to the Holy Trinity, but the Cross Kirk received its common name because *"that glorious cross"* was discovered nearby. The cross and the relics of St Nicholas soon became a talking point, particularly since they were now endorsed by both Church and Monarchy.

There are no extant records of the earliest pilgrimages but successive kings sent grants to *"the Keeper of the Holy Cross at Peebles"*. The first reference to the Hospital of St Leonard and Lawrence at Eshiels – actually a hospice for pilgrims – is dated 1327, when the Burgh bailies paid 30 shillings (about £80 in today's money)[15] to the Master of the hospital.[16] This

---

[14] This section is substantially informed by CB Gunn, *The Church and Monastery of the Holy Cross of Peebles,* James Lewis, Selkirk, 1909; R Renwick, *A Peebles Aisle and Monastery*, Carson and Nicol, Glasgow, 1897

[15] Conversions to 2015 values are rough guides for comparative purposes. They are based on the currency calculators at www.nationalarchives.gov.uk/currency/results and www.thisismoney.co.uk divided by 12 to reflect Scottish values .

[16] Robert Renwick, *Peebles: Burgh and Parish in Early History*, Peebles, A Redpath, 1903

shows that pilgrims were by then arriving in significant numbers.

The Burgh account of 1327-8 records an annual fee of £7 (equivalent to more than £390) to the keeper of the Holy Cross and there were frequent gifts of money and land from monarchs, nobles and town burgers. The high altar functioned as a kind of finance desk where deals, loans and mortgages were agreed between the various parties. The church became an important place of pilgrimage with its custom-made shrine built on the site where the urn had been found. An arched aperture in the south wall enabled the relics to be viewed from both inside and outside the church.

THE TRINITARIAN FRIARS

The Order of the Most Holy Trinity and of the Captives *Ordo Sanctissimae Trinitatis et Captivorum* was founded by St. John de Matha in the area of Cerfroid, some 80 km northeast of Paris. Known as the Trinitarians or Red Friars, the order was approved by Pope Innocent III in December 1198. One third of its income was dedicated to ransom Christians captured during the Crusades. And every community of Trinitarians also provided hospitality and education and looked after the sick and poor of the area.

The monks or friars wore a white outer garment with a red and blue cross on the breast. Their cloaks had a cross on the left shoulder. They took vows of extreme poverty and lived on charity. Barred even from riding horses, they used asses for transport. The superior was addressed as Minister.

By the time of the Reformation, eleven Trinitarian churches or friaries had been founded in Scotland - at Aberdeen, Berwick, Brechin, Cromarty, Dunbar, Dundee, Durnoch, Failford, Houston, Peebles, and – Scotlandwell, although several were destroyed over the years by invading English armies.

Initially the Cross Kirk was looked after by two Trinitarian friars and by 1448 a small community of Trinitarian friars was in residence.[17] Then, in 1473 King James III and Queen Margaret, backed by the king's uncle, Louis XI of France, successfully petitioned Brother Robert, Head of the Order in Paris for agreement to erect a monastery at the Cross Kirk. The new establishment was endowed with the Trinitarian monastery of Beruic (Berwick), which had been destroyed by the English, and the parish church of Ketnes (Kettins) in Perthshire. Brother Robert appointed a friar by the name of John Blenk as the monastery's first Minister.

John Blenk was duly inducted as Minister by the Vicar of Peebles, Alexander Burgan, on 12 April 1474. The ceremony involved touching the church door and receiving the keys, chalice, Bible and other ornaments from the altar. The imposing west tower of the Cross Kirk, along with domestic buildings and a cloister were added around this time and from then until the Reformation the church was home to a small community of friars in their distinctive white habits emblazoned on the front with a blue and red cross.

Excavations by the Office of Works in 1923 exposed foundations of the cloisters and monastic buildings. These

---

[17] Pevsner Architectural Guides, The Buildings of Scotland Borders, Cruft, Dunbar and Fawcett, Yale University Press, 2006, p613

were built on the north side of the church - in contrast to most religious houses which erected all their facilities to the south. This is probably because the shrine and its relics were on the south wall of the church. It meant that the friars' domestic quarters would have been in the shade for much of the day and exposed to the cold north wind.

A PLACE OF PILGRIMAGE

A very public miracle added greatly to the fame of the church and its relics. This took place during Beltane in 1474 - less than a month after John Blenk's arrival as the first Minister. The town was *en fête* for the annual Beltane festival and huge crowds thronged the town. At the Cross Kirk the relic was about to be held aloft when a plume of black smoke was seen over the town: a house in the Brygat (modern Bridgegate) was ablaze. The ceremony went ahead and the fire was miraculously doused.[18] The house owners, John Scot and his wife Alyson bestowed on the church a payment of 12 pence a year (about £3) from their property in the Brygat because their home *"was kepyt fra byrnyng with felon (fierce) fyr fro the tym furth that the haly crois was schawyng".*[19]

Regular visits by Scottish royalty and nobility, particularly in the 15th and 16th centuries ensured that Peebles and its

---

[18] C.B Gunn Op Cit, p17

[19] The Scottish Burgh Records Society, *Charters and Documents and Extracts from Records, Burgh of Peebles, 1165-1710*, Edinburgh, 1872, p172

church of the Holy Cross remained one of the most significant of Scottish pilgrim destinations.[20]

Beltane was probably the most popular feast day, with the chance to mix physical with spiritual pursuits by joining in the fun of a long-established fair. The poem Peebles to the Play, believed to be written by King James I (1394-1437), tells a story around the town's major festival and its revels, quarrels, "*dancing and deray*" and rustic love-making - and alludes to its relic.

The poem opens with the lines:

"At Beltane when ilk body's bound[21]

To Peblis to the Play"

The whole neighbourhood turns out:

"Hope-Kailzie and Cardrona

Gathered out thickfold..."

---

[20] Steve Boardman & Eila Williamson, *The Cult of Saints and the Virgin Mary in Medieval Scotland*, Boydell & Brewer, 2010 p180

[21] *"Ilk body's bound"*: everyone's on their way

And in the penultimate stanza a character swears by *"the Haly Rood of Peblis"*.[22]

Beltane at Peebles was one of the most popular pilgrimages of medieval Scotland. Well before the church became an abbey, two hostels had been built to accommodate the pilgrims – one at Eshiels and the other in the town itself at the west end of the High Street. By the 16th century there were

The Feast of the Finding of the Cross, called Beltane, in 1496, as imagined by Alex Blackwood

two Holy Fairs each lasting two days – the Feast of the Finding of the Cross at Beltane and the feast of the Exaltation of the Cross in September. The hostels were full and the open spaces around the Cross Kirk, particularly on the south side within sight of the shrine, were crowded with campers.

---

[22] C.B. Gunn (translator), *Peebles to the Play*, Selkirk, James Lewis, 1904

One of the regular pilgrims was James IV who always gave a handsome cash donation and mixed piety with pleasure in pursuit of sport and game. In 1505 he gave the Cross Kirk four ounces (112 grams) of gold to decorate the relic as well as a series of cash donations - and 12 pence (about £3) in "spur silver", paid to the choristers, for the disturbance caused by his spurs clanking on the

James IV

stone floor when he arrived late for worship. Regular visits and donations continued the following year and in 1507 he went a step further. On 30 April he commissioned a golden cross with a silver base. It was duly delivered on 16 February 1508. The cost in gold, silver and labour was £19.2s.3d – more than £1,665 today.

One of the days chosen for veneration, first mentioned in a document relating to the mills of Peebles in 1506,[23] was 14 September, the feast day of the Exaltation or Elevation of the Holy Cross - otherwise known as Holyrood or Halyrude Day.

This feast day dates back to 7th century Rome and commemorates the recovery of the Holy Cross, said to have been discovered in the year 326 by Helena, mother of Constantine the Great, who entrusted it to the Bishop of Jerusalem. Pilgrims carried away small pieces but it was found that, miraculously, it never got smaller! The Persians

---

[23] C.B. Gunn Op Cit, *The Church and Monastery of the Holy Cross of Peebles,* p23

carried it off when they captured Jerusalem in 614 but it was recovered and returned to Jerusalem by the Byzantine Emperor Heraclius in 629. The choice of this feast day for the veneration of the relics at Peebles may have been why people came to believe that the relics included a piece of the "true cross" as there is no record of it arriving here – an event that would certainly have been worthy of a mention. The Feast of the Finding of the Holy Cross of Peebles, was moved from Beltane to a slightly later date - 15 May in 1530 -probably to avoid the clash with the raucous and decidedly non-religious Beltane celebrations.

James V

Royal patronage continued to enrich the assets and reputation of the Cross Kirk. James V (who was not even three years old when his father was killed at Flodden in 1513) was a regular visitor who donated useful amounts of cash. He went further in 1529. In a letter to the friars he granted the Cross Kirk the house and revenues of the Trinitarian church at Dunbar as long as one of the friars lived and took Divine Service there. This letter describes the Cross Kirk as the place *"where a part of the very Cross that our Salvator was crucified on is honoured and kept."*[24] It is the first – and only - reference to the "true cross" at Peebles. It could be a 19-year-old's mistake, or he may have presented the relic to the monastery.

---

[24] C.B. Gunn Op Cit p27

James V's wife (and later widow) Marie de Lorraine, better known as Mary of Guise, was equally in thrall to the Cross Kirk. A note in her own handwriting shows the importance of Peebles as a place of pilgrimage shortly before the Reformation.[25]

Mary of Guise

It is thought that the note was written in 1541 or 1542 before the birth of Mary Queen of Scots as it sets out her wishes should she die without being able to make pilgrimages to seven shrines in continental Europe and three in Scotland. The Scottish shrines are St Trygrian (probably St Ninian's in Whithorn), St Adrian of "the May Island' (St Adrian's Priory - a shrine for barren women) and "*la Vree Crois de Pieble*" - the True Cross at Peebles. At the age of 27 she had already been married and widowed twice, and lost four children in infancy. No wonder she was wary of death.

Marie intended to make an offering at each shrine, and to sponsor a High Mass, with an offering of wax of the weight of

[25] Marguerite Wood, editor, *The Balcarres Papers and the Foreign Correspondence of Marie de Lorrain*, Scottish History Society, 1923, pp78 & 79

a child of four months - the heaviest possible. She asks her mother to perform these rituals in the event of her death.

CHANGES

Mary, who later became Regent of Scotland on behalf of her baby daughter, was an upper class of pilgrim. There were many others of less substantial means begging heavenly help for personal and family problems, illness and disabilities. But the days of pilgrimage, and not just at the Cross Kirk, were soon to end – or rather become subject to a proscriptive ban. Such superstitious stuff, let alone the veneration of "holy relics", was condemned as idolatry when a stern Reformation increasingly took hold in Scotland.

Another attack by an English army in 1549 was a sign of what was to come. The soldiers rampaged through Peebles, sacked the town and set fire to the buildings. They wrecked the parish church beyond repair and burnt the Cross Kirk. It was part of a deliberate policy of attrition lasting more than nine years in what later became known as the Rough Wooing.

The ruins of St Andrews church by Francis Grose, 1790

The aim had been to force a marriage between Henry VIII's son Edward VI, now two years into his reign, and the infant Mary Queen of Scots. But the now fiercely committed

Protestant English administration and its equally committed army also took the chance to spread the ideas of the Reformation.

Scotland was already astir with challenges to Papal authority. Leading Protestants were burnt at the stake, Cardinal Beaton was murdered, and there was increasing conflict between the Catholic monarchy and the common people.

In 1557 some of the Protestant lords formed the Congregation of Christ, the Lords Congregation. The aim, as they put it, was to *"establish the most blessed word of God."* They were backed by soldiers and their own armed retainers.

Rioting broke out as John Knox and other reformers stirred up popular feelings against Church and State, personified by the Catholic regent Mary of Guise (and later her daughter Mary

John Knox preaching before the Lords Congregation

Queen of Scots - at this time still in France and married to the heir to the French throne). Across the border in England, the Catholic Mary Tudor, who died in 1558, was succeeded by her Protestant half-sister Elizabeth, who sent military aid to assist an armed uprising by the Lords Congregation. Reform appeared unstoppable and anyone acquainted with the fate of the English monasteries could guess what might happen next.[26]

The friars in the Cross Kirk must have faced the upheavals with great trepidation. The Minister since 1552, Gilbert Broun or Brown, had to repair buildings burned by the English army amid growing uncertainty over the future. His predecessor, James Paterson, had already begun to sell off abbey land – restoring a property given to the Cross Kirk by Sir Patrick Heburn of Waughton, a privy councillor, to a younger son also called Patrick.[27]

As well as repairing the church building, Gilbert Brown wanted to make sure that he and his fellow friars were not turned out penniless onto unforgiving streets.

There were plenty of men with money ready to do business, not least the powerful William Hay, the 5th Lord of Yester and Provost of Peebles, at Neidpath Castle.

[26] Plantagenet & Fiona Somerset Fry, *The History of Scotland* Routledge & Kegan Paul, 1982, pp134-135

[27] C.B Gunn Op Cit p32

Across Scotland, lords and lesser landowners saw the opportunity to expand their estates with the addition of Church property. Faced with dispersal, the friars made sure they secured adequate provision for themselves – a practice that was already commonplace elsewhere. On 30 June 1556 Gilbert Brown conveyed to Robert Brown, son of John Brown, and probably related, seven acres of Floors on payment of £3.17s a year – about £88 in today's money.[28] This included five and a half acres of land near Eshiels that had been gifted to the Cross Kirk by James, Earl of Morton, in 1460. The land was conveyed outright on 2 July 1559.[29]

On 10 November 1558 Friar Gilbert Brown granted Cross Kirk land in Kettins to James Small, the tenant, *"for the sum of three hundred merks* (worth more than £435 today) *paid in reparation of his Place burned by the English"*. The transaction included feu-ferme (an annual rent) of £8, about £157 today, and a condition that James Small would entertain the Minister, friars and their servants whenever they went there to collect the teinds or tithes of Kettins church.[30] Friar Brown had no right to seal this transaction, and we have no way of knowing whether he used this substantial sum of money on church repairs.

As the Scottish Reformation gathered pace, Friar Brown, with the agreement of his four fellow friars made a deal with Lord Hay of Yester, one of the principal landowners in the area. On

---

[28] Ibid, p35 ;

[29] Ibid p 26

[30] Ibid, p37

5 July 1559, in exchange for Lord Hay's undertaking to *"maintene and defend the said minister and convent, their cornes, medois, and guides* (corn, meadows and goods) *moveable and unmoveable"* the friars agreed that if they were not allowed to enjoy their abbey *"peacabille of the auld manner"*, he, Lord Hay, would have first refusal of whatever they could dispose of – *"he payand thairfor as utheris will do"*.[31]

DISSOLUTION

The end was getting nearer. There were numerous disturbances across Scotland. Peebles was on full alert and in March 1560 a detachment of the Lords Congregation army led by John, Master of Maxwell, arrived in Peebles and took possession of the Cross Kirk.[32]

A *"trembling and fearing"* Gilbert Brown told some of the town leaders on 30 March 1560 that *"for fear of his life and the destruction of his place and monastery"* he had *"changed his dress by changing his white habit for a gray keltour gowne and putting on a how black bonnet but not from any hatred of his old religion"* when he heard that the Reformers' army was on its way.[33]

---

[31] R. Renwick, *A Peebles Aisle and Monastery*, Glasgow: Carson & Nicol, 1897, p37

[32] R. Renwick, *Peebles during the Reign of Queen Mary*, The Neidpath Press, 1803, p75

[33] Op cit The Scottish Burgh Records Society, p259

The whole town was uneasy. Orders were issued to suppress any *"fray or suddand tulye"* [quarrel or brawl]. Penalties were imposed on anyone who drew a weapon on any bailie or officer in the execution of his duty.[34]

In August 1560 the Scottish Parliament formally abolished the Catholic Mass and recognised the reformed faith of Protestantism. And before the year was out, the Secret (or Privy) Council ordered Gilbert Brown to hand over the Cross Kirk as a replacement parish church because St Andrew's was deemed irreparable. He and his four fellow friars were forced to leave and the church property sold off bit by bit.

Pilgrims continued to arrive for many years. In 1580 the General Assembly of the Kirk of Scotland urged the government to suppress pilgrimages to *"wells and kirks"* and asked in particular for punishment of *"them that passed latelie to the Haly Rud of Peibles."* [35] By 1599 names were being noted and sent to the pilgrims' home parishes for action to be taken against them. Finally, at Beltane on 14 May 1601 the Minister and the bailies of Peebles reported for the first time that *"there was no resorting of people into the Cross Kirk to commit any sign of superstition there."*[36]

---

[34] James Walter Buchan, *History of Peeblesshire*, Jackson, Wylie & Co., Glasgow,1925, Vol II, p24

[35] J.W. Buchan Op Cit, Vol I, p 65

[36] C.B. Gunn, *The Book of the Cross Kirk, Peebles, A.D. 1560-1690, Presbytery and Episcopacy*, Neidpath Pressm 1912, pp58-59

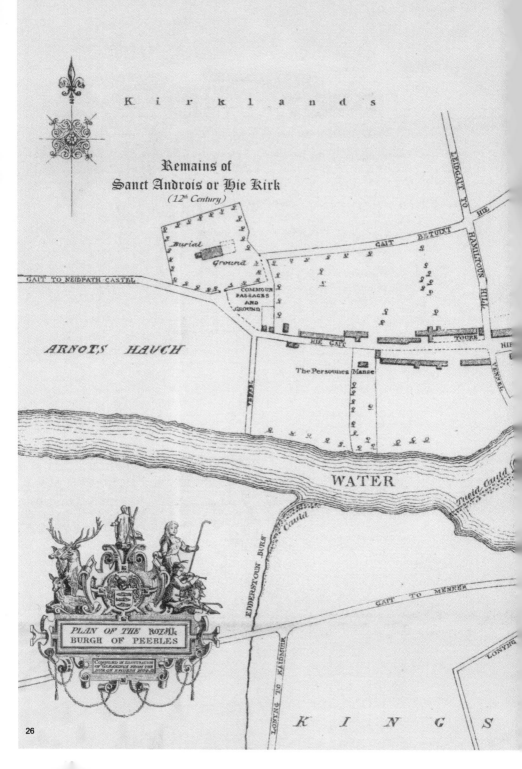

K i r k l a n d s

Remains of
Sanct Androis or Hie Kirk
(12ᵗʰ Century)

GAIT BETUIXT

LEIDGAIT TO HIE

HAMILTOUN HILL

Burial

Ground

GAIT TO NEIDPATH CASTEL

COMMOUN
PASSAGES
AND
GROUND

ARNOT'S HAUCH

HIE GAIT

TOURS

HI

VENN

The Persounes Manse

WATER

Tueia Cauld

Caula

EDDERSTOUN BURN

PLAN OF THE ROYAL
BURGH OF PEEBLES

COMPILED IN ILLUSTRATION
OF GLEANINGS FROM THE
BURGH RECORDS 1604-54

GAIT TO MENEER

LONYNG TO KAIDMUIR

LONYNG

K I N G S

26

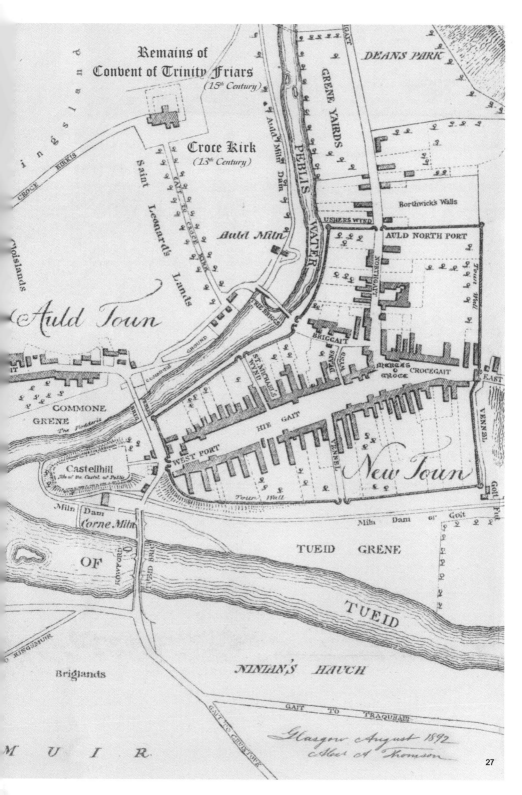

Remains of
Convent of Trinity Friars
(15ᵗʰ Century)

DEANS PARK

Croce Kirk
(13ᵗʰ Century)

GRENE YAIRDS

PEBLIS WATER

USHERS WYND

Borthwick's Walls

Auld Miln

AULD NORTH PORT

Saint Leonards Lands

GAIT TO CROCE KIRK

Auld Miln Dam

NORTHGAIT

Town Wall

Auld Toun

CROCE KIRK'S

Moislands

GROUND

BRIGGAIT

MERCAS & CROCE

CROCEGAIT

EAST

ST MICHAELS WYND

DEANS SYNDE

GRAY

HIE GAIT

New Toun

COMMONE GRENE

The Floddoris

WEST PORT

FENNEL

VENNEL

Goit Fid

Castellhill
Sle of the Castel of Pebly

Town Wall

Miln Dam
Corne Miln

Miln Dam or Goit

TUEID GRENE

OF

TUEID BRIG

RONFORD

TUEID

Brigiands

NINIAN'S HAUCH

KINGSMUIR

GAIT TO TRAQUHAIR

GAIT TO CHURTOUN

M U I R.

Glasgow August 1892
Alex A Thomson

27

PARISH CHURCH

The Cross Kirk's role as parish church was to last until 1778. Under the new Presbyterian rule the three altars – the Black Rood or High Altar and those dedicated to the Holy Blood and St Sebastian – were dismantled. Over time a pulpit, seats and a gallery were built. In 1656 the chancel was demolished and the building shortened some 30 feet (about 9 metres) by the construction of a new wall and doorway in the east end. The change was marked by an inscription over the new east door.

Two burial aisles were added onto the south wall and one on the north. The north aisle cut across the line of the cloisters. These, together with the monastic apartments, were used to accommodate victims of the plague in 1666. Some became school-rooms and homes for teachers up to the beginning of the 18th century. They gradually decayed through lack of maintenance and repairs until they became unstable and the stones were recycled as building material. By the end of the 18th century nothing was left of the monastic buildings.

The last communion in the Cross Kirk took place in 1778 after a new parish church was built in a more convenient location at the west end of the High Street. The Cross Kirk was abandoned in 1784 and stripped of its roof and furniture. In 1789 the church walls were bought by a builder for use as building material. There was a public outcry and the council stopped the sale and declared that the building should remain in its then state *"for all time coming"*. Despite this, much of the south wall is known to have fallen by 1811.[37] In 1809, by which time the land was owned by the Duke of Queensbury, a

---

[37] RCAHMS Op cit p204

request to use the churchyard as a coal depot was approved by the Duke and the council. Fortunately, it was never pursued. The Ministry of Works took over the site in 1925 and it is now cared for by Historic Environment Scotland.

THE CROSS KIRK TODAY - the ruins

The site was extensively quarried following the construction of the new parish church at the west end of the High Street in 1784. What is left are substantial remnants of the 13th century nave and 15th century tower, together with some foundations of domestic buildings and outlines of the cloisters and other rooms.

The 13th century church was basically a rectangular structure of whinstone with buff sandstone dressings, and a sacristy that projected near the east end of the north wall. A chamfered base course ran around the exterior and there was a string course below the windows, some of which originally were traceried.

The tower, added after 1474 when the church became a monastery, had five storeys and was 50 feet (15.25 metres) high, although the east wall is now reduced to first floor level. The tower was built of rubble with sandstone quoins, which are absent in the upper 15 feet (4.5 metres). This suggests that this part of the tower was rebuilt at some time, perhaps after the church was burned by the English army in 1549. One of the Hutton sketches shows that there was a corbelled parapet at the summit.

A canopied niche ten feet above ground in the south-west corner of the tower once held a statue - probably an image of St Nicholas.

Cross Church, Peebles, S.W. view, 1796

Sketches from 1790 onwards show the domestic buildings and church roof had already disappeared by then.

When it was built the church resembled the now also ruined parish church of St Andrew about a quarter of a mile away, which was dedicated in 1195. The building was about the same size - 102 feet (31 metres) long and 26 feet (eight metres) wide. The walls were more than three feet (one metre) thick and 24 feet (seven metres) high. Doorways and windows were often dressed with yellow sandstone.

South door of the Cross Church at Peebles, 1796

Only the north wall of the nave remains at its original height. The eastern end of the south wall is reasonably complete but only the lowest courses remain of the western end, where a modern wall serves as a boundary to the burial ground of the Hay family of Haystoun. There were once two burial aisles in the south wall. The western one has completely disappeared. The other, now ruinous and inaccessible, was probably built in 1705 after the death of Lady Anne Douglas, daughter of the Earl of Morton. First known as the Morton Aisle, it later came into the possession of the Erskine family of Smithfield and Venlaw.[38] The burial aisle of the Earls of March on the north wall is in a better condition, roofed, and is used as a (locked) store. All three aisles were built after the demise of the monastery.

Writing in 1790, Dr William Dalgleish said there were *"four, if not five"* windows in the south wall, each 15 feet (4.5 metres) tall.[39] Three of these were in the nave and two in the chancel. All but one has disappeared and the lower half of this has been blocked up and much altered.

The west gable rises to its full height where it joins the north wall of the nave, the remainder being level with the first floor of the tower.

---

[38] C.B. Gunn, *The Manual of the Cross Kirk*, Neidpath Press, 1914, p68

[39] Op cit Renwick, Aisle and Monastery, p48, quoting National Library of Scotland MS. 29.4.2 (Hutton Collection) vol. lv, letter dated 24 May 1790

Most of the walls of the chancel and sacristy are reduced to their lowest courses, and have disappeared in places. They were cut off from the church after the Reformation, when a new wall with a large arched window was built where the rood screen once

Inscription over "new" doorway- FEIRE GOD 1656

stood. The lintel over the central doorway of this wall is inscribed with the words FEIRE GOD 1656. It is thought the wall was built with stones from the monastic quarters. This 17th century wall seems to have been built on the foundations of a pulpitum which had an altar recessed into it each side of the door.[40]

The excavated cist grave at the site of the shrine © HES

There is now no trace of the shrine. It was no doubt destroyed, along with its contents, at the Reformation.

The Morton, or Erskine, burial aisle later obscured its location. But the excavations of 1923 revealed a "grave-like cavity" below the south wall aligned roughly north-east to south-

---

[40] Ian C. Hannah, *Screens and Lofts in Scottish Churches*,
Proceedings of the Society of Antiquaries of Scotland, Vol 70, 1936.

west.[41] Archaeologists decided this was probably a Bronze Age cist, or coffin-like stone box or ossuary used to hold the bones of the dead.

The cavity also contained fragments of a sculptured stone slab, now mounted in a frame and kept at the Tweeddale Museum in Peebles High Street.

The image is thought to represent a bishop, but the lettering is of a type found on monuments carved no earlier than 1480, which suggests this may have been part of later restoration work on the original shrine.

In addition there appeared to be the foundations of another altar, although only three were ever recorded.

How the stone might have looked, by F.A. Greenhill © HES

The stones of the main west door, now the inner doorway of the tower, are mostly intact and there are the remains of three other doorways, now blocked, in the south wall, one of which was the original church entrance. Of two doorways in the north wall, one is the entrance of the burial aisle of the Douglas Earls of March and the other gave access to the

---

[41] Op Cit RCAHMS p207

cloisters and other monastic buildings and was probably added when the church became an abbey.

Dr. William Dalgleish, Minister of Peebles Parish Church, who wrote the section about Peebles in the 1794 Statistical Account of Scotland, found the church almost complete except for its roof, though the monastery's domestic buildings had long since been dismantled for their stone. A contemporary sketch of the main west door shows that quarrying for stone had begun soon after it ceased to be the parish church.

A description of Peebles in a gazetteer of the principal towns of Scotland in 1828 noted *"the ruins of Cross-Kirk, built by Alexander the Third, in 1257, dedicated to the Holy Cross, and Saint Nicholas; the steeple of this church is also entire. Alexander built a house contiguous to this church, for himself, which continued for ages to be a royal residence. It was here the Poem of 'Peebles to the Play' was written, in which is described, many of the diversions and festivals of the times, by James the First."*[42]

By the late 1800s Cross Kirk was being described as a fragmentary ruin in a fir plantation on the western edge of Peebles, having a *"very desolate appearance"*.[43] The Burgh acquired the whole site in 1917 and it came under guardianship of the Department of Environment in 1925

---

[42] Anon, *A Descriptive Account of the Principal Towns in Scotland to accompany Wood's Town Atlas*, Edinburgh, 1828

[43] D. MacGibbon & T Ross, *The ecclesiastical architecture of Scotland, Vol 3,* D. Douglas, Edinburgh, 1896, p482

following the excavations of 1923. It is now cared for by Historic Environment Scotland.

The work of Robert Renwick and Clement Bryce Gunn in researching and writing up the history of the Cross Kirk and drawing attention to its importance in the history of Peebles was crucial in securing the future of the site.

Clement Bryce Gunn surveys the ivy-clad ruins c1908

The Cross Kirk from the north

TIMELINE

1261: A *"stately and venerable cross"* is found at Peebles but *"it is quite unknown in what year and by what persons it was hidden there."* People believe it was hidden there around the year 296. Shortly afterwards a *"stone urn"* is found a few paces away. It contains the ashes and bones of a man *"torn limb from limb"*. He is assumed to be the man whose name is carved on the stone *"wherein that holy cross was lying"* – Bishop Saint Nicholas.

1296: Friar Thomas, Master of the House of the Holy Cross is one of a dozen civic and church leaders who swear loyalty and pay homage to King Edward I of England at the castle in

Peebles,[44] which stood where the parish church with its crown steeple now dominates the western end of the High Street. Edward is there at the head of his army in the first of a 60-year series of invasions in what later became known as the Wars of Scottish Independence.

1327: The Exchequer Rolls record a grant of £7 (worth about £370 today) to the Keeper of the Holy Cross at Peebles for his yearly fee. Similar payments are made in 1328, 1329 and 1330. In 1331 and 1332 the payment is £6.13s (about £340) and in 1348 20s (£50) was paid *"as part of the pension that used to be paid"*.

1390: King Robert II gives land at Kingsmeadows to *"the church of the Haly Rude"* at Peebles and to Friar Thomas, the king's chaplain, and his successors serving the same office in the church.

c1430: The humorous poem *Peebles to the Play* is written by King James I. The penultimate stanza contains the line *"By the Haly Rude of Peblis, I may not rest for greeting"*.

1431: Walter Scott, Lord of Buccleuch, agrees to repay a loan of £100 (worth more than £5,200 today) any day between sunrise and sunset upon the high altar of the church of the Holy Cross of Peebles.

1456: A meeting of the Burgh Court on 13 December agrees to a request to present Friar John Jameson to the place and living of the *"Cors Kyrk"* after he swears by his priesthood not to give bribes to any man out of the goods belonging to the

---

[44] Op Cit C. B. Gunn, Manual, p5

Cross Church. He is allowed to take his living out of the church revenues and spend the rest as needed either on the church or on the relic. The Burgh had the right to present the Minister of the church.

1458: The grant of Kingsmeadows is confirmed by King James II.

1460: James, Earl of Morton, gives the Cross Kirk 5.5 acres (2.23 hectares) of land in Eshiels.

c1460: The date of the poem or play *The Three Tales of the Three Priests of Peebles*, written by an unknown author. The priests or friars meet in the Virgin Inn, at the Old Town end of Brig House Knowe, modern Biggiesknowe, on St Brides Day (1 February).

1461: James II's queen, Mary of Guelders, visits the Cross Kirk and donates ten shillings (about £28).

1462: The Burgh Court *"decretyt and gaf thair lectioun"* [decreed and elected] on 8 November Friar Thomas Lorymar to serve in the Cross Kirk until Beltane – despite objections from eight burghers.

1464: On 1 October, Friar William Gibson, master of the Cross Kirk, and his *"for-speaker"* William of Peebles asks the Burgh Court *"for the reverans of God and our Lady and the heile of their saullis"* for a piece of land under the east end of Castlehill on the north side between the gate and the hill so that Friar William, with the help of Christian people, can build a house of alms to harbour the poor for *"saull heile"* [soul-heal]. The Court agrees and goes immediately to the land in question, where Bailie William Dickson takes earth and stone and places it in Friar William's hands – the traditional way of conveying land from one owner to the next.

1474: On 3 February Brother Robert, head of the order of Trinity Friars, agrees to the request of King James III and his queen Margaret, backed by Louis XI of France for permission to erect a monastery at the Cross Kirk. Brother Robert also annexes the Trinity Friars monastery at Berwick, which had been destroyed by the English, and the parish church of Kettins, Forfarshire, to the Cross Kirk. Friar John Blenk is appointed Minister of the three churches and Brother Robert says he will resign his right to appoint the minister as soon as there were enough friars at Peebles.

1474: On 12 April John Blenk is inducted as head minister. Work soon begins on building the monastic buildings.

1474: The miracle of the Elevation of the Cross during Beltane in early May is confirmed in the Burgh Court by John Scott and his wife Alison on 18 July. They hand Bailie John Dickson a penny (about 25p), and promise 12 pence (about £3) annually to the Holy Cross out of their land in the Brygait (Bridgegate) because their burning house was saved at the moment the Holy Cross was shown to the pilgrims at the Cross Kirk.

1481: Sir Walter Scott, Lord of Buccleuch, buried in the Cross Kirk, one of six or seven of his title buried there.[45]

---

[45] Op Cit Buchan, Vol III, p185

1484: The Cross Kirk Minister, Friar John Mador, and two other friars, sitting in chapter on 18 December, promise Thomas Hay, *"sheref deput of Peblis"* and Cristiane Dudingston, his spouse, to celebrate mass every day at the Black Rood altar in the Cross Kirk and pay five shillings (about £15) for every day they miss. This is a response to frequent gifts of property and money. A few days later, on 31 December, the couple grant their land and home in Old Town to support masses at the Black Rood altar for the souls of donors.

1488: The 16-year-old King James IV inaugurates his reign with the first of a series of pilgrimages to the Cross Kirk on 22 November to do penance for his part in the death of his father. He gives the church 18 shillings (more than £50).

The seal of Cross Kirk Minister John Mador shows the south side of the church, still without a tower, behind a large cross. The legend reads: S commune ecclie sancte crucis de peblis.

1492: The will, dated 9 February, of David Scott of Buccleugh directs that his body is buried in the Cross Kirk. He dies the same year.

1492: Four shillings (about £11) annual rent is given by William of Dunsyre to Robert Tonnok, chaplain of the Holy

Blood altar at the Cross Kirk, on 3 March for a mass every year in honour of the Holy Blood and for William's soul-heal.

1494: On 31 May Peebles burgher John Mador gives his son William Mador, one of the friars, his land tenement and *biggin* [building] on the south side of the High Street and William immediately resigns ownership to Thomas Eumond and his wife Christian.

1502: James IV visits on 6 May and 18 September, giving the Cross Kirk 18 shillings (about £50) on both occasions.

1503: A burgess called Gilbert Williamson gives rent of eight shillings (about £23) from land and tenement in Northgate to the Cross Kirk Minister Friar Thomas Lowis on 9 October. In return the friary will hold annual services on the anniversary of William's death for the benefit of William and his wife Janet Middlemass. In default he or his heirs would take back the rent and give it to the chaplains at the parish church.

Seal of Thomas Lowis

1504-1508: James IV is a frequent visitor, stopping at Peebles and visiting the Cross Kirk several times every year. On 27 May 1505 he gives the Cross Kirk four ounces (113.4 grams) of gold. *"Spur silver"*, generally 12 pennies (about £3) is also frequently paid during these years for the disturbance caused by the King's spurs clanking on the stone floor when he arrives late for a service.

1507: The King donates 14 shillings (£40) and an honorarium to the friars of 40 shillings (£110). He also commissions a gold cross for the Cross Kirk. It is made by the goldsmith Matthew Auchleck and duly delivered on 16 February 1508. It weighs 7.5 ounces (212.6 grams) and has a base of silver weighing 4.25 ounces (120.5 grams). The total cost is more than £1,700 in today's money.

1510: The first – and only – reference to the *"abbey of the Trinity called the Cross Kirk in Peblis"* in a document recording an annual rent of ten shillings (£28) for two anniversary services every year for the father and mother of one of the friars.

1529: King James V grants the monastery the house and revenue of the Order of the Holy Trinity at Dunbar. The same letter to the friars, dated 1 July, 1529, describes the Cross Kirk as the place *"where a part of the very Cross that our Salvator was crucified on is honoured and kept,"*[46] This is the first and only reference to the "true cross".

1530: The Archbishop of Glasgow names 15 May for the annual double – two-day - feast of the Finding of the Holy Cross of the Ministry of Peebles.

1560: 7 December. The Secret Council in Edinburgh agrees to the Burgh Council's request to make the Cross Kirk the Parish Church of Peebles. Not everyone was happy with the change. Rural parishioners petitioned the council against it, and Thomas Hay, Master of Yester, demanded that it should

---

[46] C.B Gunn Op Cit p28

not prejudice the title to the kirk buildings that he obtained from Gilbert Brown.[47]

1564: Former Minister Gilbert Brown complains that his pension and those of the other friars were in arrears and suggests selling the *"ornaments, vestments and jewels"* in safe keeping at Neidpath Castle and Chapelhill to meet the arrears. Five men are appointed to investigate. Nothing more is heard of the Cross Kirk treasures.[48]

1602: The parson is instructed to arrest those that *"superstitiously repair"* to the Cross Kirk at Beltane for punishment by the magistrate.[49]

1621: Conveyance of the Cross Kirk to the Burgh Council is confirmed by Royal Charter signed by James VI.

1623: A sheep thief is executed by drowning for sheep stealing, including a ewe from the cloister of the Cross Kirk.

1624: August 20: One hundred men turn out for *"a general muster and weaponshawing[50] in the Croce Kirkyeard."* Musters continue to be held there for many years. In the same

---

[47] Op Cit The Scottish Burgh Records Society, p267-168. See p27above

[48] C.B. Gunn, The Book of the Cross Kirk, Presbytery and Episcopacy, Neidpath Press, 1912, p20-21

[49] Ibid, p70; Op Cit Buchan, Vol 2, p320n

[50] Show of weapons

year, all the Cross Kirk property not mentioned in the 1621 charter is granted to John, Lord Hay of Yester.

1626-1640: Workmen are paid varying amounts by the Burgh for removing stone and slates from the Cross Kirk for repairs to the Chapel of the Virgin Mary in the town and the Tweed Bridge.

1637: A slater named John Speir is paid £44.7s (about £500 today) for repairs to the Cross Kirk during the preceding year.

1643: More repairs to the church.

1645-6: Plague in Peebles. Trees cut down in the Cross Kirk grounds to build two lodges to accommodate victims, whose clothes were burnt in a kiln on the site.[51]

1649: Merchants start to build themselves seats in areas of the church reserved for magistrates, the council and leading families.

1653: The Burgh Council agrees to build two pews and add to the magistrates' seat and says any burgesses or freemen can club together and build pews for themselves.

1666: Plague victims are put into cells and vaults in the former conventual buildings.

1776: The Minister, William Dalgleish calls for a new parish church as the Cross Kirk is semi-ruinous and inconveniently situated, with access roads frequently blocked with snow.

---

[51] Op Cit Gunn, Presbytery and Episcopacy, p130

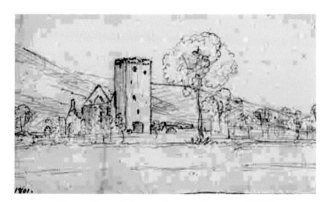
Cross Church from the north-west, 1801

1778: The Council agrees to contribute towards a new church at the west end of the High Street.

1783: The last communion in the Cross Kirk.

1784: The Cross Kirk is abandoned and the roof removed.

1789: The magistrates sell the church to a builder to quarry the stone. The builder pulls out of the sale after a public outcry and the council later decrees that the church should remain in its then condition *"in all time coming".*

1809: The Burgh Council agrees to a request to turn the site of the Cross Kirk into a coal yard, with the agreement of the owner, the Duke of Queensberry. Fortunately the coal merchant finds an alternative site.

1817: The council agrees to a request by John Hay to repair the walls and "*ornament the ground*" on condition that they should become his property, Hay observes that the ruin would otherwise "*fall into complete decay*".

1917: The Hay family give the Cross Kirk to the Council after buying the surrounding ground from the Earl of Wemyss for £120 – about £6,000 in today's money.

1923: The Cross Kirk site is excavated by the Ministry of Works and the ruins consolidated.

1925: The Cross Kirk is brought under State control.

APPENDIX ONE: **THE NEITAN STONE**

This inscribed boulder, shaped like a kite, is thought to be an early Christian tombstone that may once have stood in the graveyard of the Cross Kirk. It is smooth and rounded and measures 19" x 8.5 inches (48 x 21.5cms), ranging in thickness from 1.75 inches to 3.5 inches (4.5 x 8.9cms). It is carved with a cross on both the front and back and probably dates to the late 7th or early 8th century.[52]

The inscription reads *Neitano Sacerdos* "(here lies) Neitan the priest" (or perhaps bishop)". Neitan is a native British (Brythonic and Pictish) name.

The Neitan Stone

It was discovered in November 1967, built into a retaining wall at the rear of the public garden in Old Town. Mr I. C. Lawson, then Secretary of the Tweeddale Society, pointed it out to

---

[52] www.canmore.org.uk/site/51521/peebles-cross-kirk

archaeologist Dr K A Steer, who recorded the stone in the journal of the Society of Antiquaries of Scotland.[53]

Until 1932, it was built into a tenement wall in the same place, which was demolished that year. Mr Lawson said he had known about it since his childhood, but no record of it had ever been published. And when the burgh was officially surveyed by staff from the Royal Commission on the Ancient and Historical Monuments of Scotland it was hidden behind a vigorous shrub. Little is known of its history but the tenement was erected about 1780, around the time the Cross Kirk was abandoned.

No one knows when it was removed or how it got to the Old Town. Most of the walls of the church were untouched for some years after it was abandoned as a place of worship, but the adjoining abbey buildings, which could have been constructed over part of the ancient graveyard, were used as a quarry for building material from the seventeenth century onwards.

The stone in the wall

The wall was demolished after the stone was discovered and the ancient gravestone was at first displayed in the Chambers Institution. It was stolen in the late 1970s or early 1980s but returned anonymously a decade later. It is once again kept in

---

[53] K.A. Steer, *Two Unrecorded Early Christian Stones*, Proceeding of the Society of Antiquaries of Scotland, Vol 101, 1968-69

the Chambers Institute, along with the remains of the bishop's medieval tombstone.

The Cross Kirk from the north-west, 2016

APPENDIX TWO **BELTANE**

The origin of this festival goes back to Celtic times. The name is thought to come from the Brythonic – early Welsh/Cornish/Breton – meaning fire (modern Welsh *tân*) of the sun god and "fire-giver", Belinus or Belenus to the early Celts.[54]

Not surprisingly, the Sun was considered sacred by human societies in early human history. Belenus was worshipped in Northern Italy, ancient Gaul and Britain. The contintental Celts equated his name with Apollo, the Greek god of prophecy, music and medicine. In Britain he featured in one of the four main festivals of the Celtic year, when, "*on the eve of May Day, the Beltain fires were lit and cattle driven between them in a purifying rite*".[55] There are more inscriptions to Belenus than to any other Celtic god.

The Peebles–born Professor John Veitch credited Cormac, Archbishop of Cashel around the year 908 as the first to mention the celebrations under the name *Beiltine*[56] and a number of writers describe the custom of lighting fires that persisted in Scotland at least to the end of the 18th century. One of the fullest descriptions was written by John Ramsay,

---

[54] John Veitch, *The History and Poetry of the Scottish Border*, William Blackwood and Sons, Vol II, Edinburgh, 1878, p211; Richard Carlyon, *A Guide to the Gods*, Heinemann/Quixote, 1981, p203

[55] Ibid, Carlyon

[56] Op Cit Veitch

Laird of Ochtertyre near Crieff, who was a patron of Robert Burns and a friend of Sir Walter Scott.

"But the most considerable of the Druidical festivals is that of Beltane, or May-day, which was lately observed in some parts of the Highlands, with extraordinary ceremonies."[57]

A contemporary description of Beltane at Peebles is found in the poem *Peebles to the Play* by King James I. The two days of raucus celebration, including a horse race with a prize of a silver bell, became one of the principal events in town. Deals were concluded, debts paid and the burgesses paraded in all their pomp and majesty.

The high jinks, which began on 3 May,[58] certainly persuaded the Cross Kirk to separate its own Feast of the Finding of the Cross from Beltane to 15 May.

The horse race was temporarily banned by the Secret Council in 1608 because it attracted *"grit numbers of people, of all qualities and ranks....betwixt whom there being quarrel, private grudges and miscontentment, it is to be ferit that, at their meeting upon fields, some troubles and inconvenients sall fall out amangs them to the break of his Majesty's peace, and disquieting of the country"*[59] It was a precautionary cancellation owing to the unsettled state of the country.

---

[57] James George Frazer, The Golden Bough (Abridged), Papermac, 1987, p617

[58] Ibid p53

[59] Op Cit James Walter Buchan, Vol 2, p40

In 1621 James VI signed a royal charter granting the Royal Burgh of Peebles the right to hold the Beltane Fair on the Tuesday before 12 May annually. The new date was to avoid interference with markets "*of greater importance*".[60]

The festival had become something of a duty by 1624 when all honest men were warned to attend "*in maist civill forme, everie men with ane sword at his belt, baith at the tyme of the Beltane fair, and horse raice upon the morne thairefter.*"[61] Non-appearance risked a fine of 40 shillings – about £22.

The date of the fair was fixed annually as 1 May in 1656 when the Burgh realised that the two days of revelry would begin that year on a Saturday, leading inexorably to "*the profanatioun of the Sabbath*".[62]

The Beltane horse race was held annually, with some breaks because of civil unrest until 1735 when there were no entrants. The council continued to pay rent for the racecourse at Whitehaugh until the proprietor Dr James Hay of Haytoun, ploughed it up in 1764. That was the end of the Beltane race.

The festival was revived in a new form 1897 to celebrate the Diamond Jubilee of Queen Victoria. The ancient custom of Riding the Marches, with a leader known as Cornet, was augmented in 1899 by the introduction of a Beltane Queen

---

[60] Peebles Beltane Festival Jubilee Book 1949, J.A. Kerr & Co, Peebles, p12

[61] Op Cit Buchan, Vol II, p41

[62] Ibid p54

coronation. Now held in June, the festival has gradually expanded over the years to become a mainly children-focussed event that involves the whole community over nine days. Since 1934 the festival has begun, weather permitting, with a religious service at the Cross Kirk. The story of the ancient site has come full circle and grounds are once again filled with people coming together in a common purpose at Beltane.

The Beltane service at the Cross Kirk, 2016 by Emma Scott

List of Sources

Anon, *A Descriptive Account of the Principal Towns in Scotland to accompany Wood's Town Atlas* (Edinburgh, 1828)

Boardman, Steve & Williamson, Ella, *The Cult of Saints and the Virgin Mary in Medieval Scotland* (Boydell & Brewer, 2010)

Buchan, J.W., *A History of Peeblesshire* (Jackson, Wylie & Co., Glasgow, 1925)

Carlyon, Richard, *A Guide to the Gods*, (Heinemann/Quixote, 1981), p203

Chambers, William, *History of Peeblesshire*, (W. & R. Chambers, Edinburgh, 1864)

Demster, Thomas, *The Ecclesiastical History of the Scottish People*, published in 1627

Frazer, James George, *The Golden Bough (abridged)*, (Papermac, 1987)

Fuller, Thomas, *Church History of Britain. Vol I* (University Press, Oxford, 1845)

Gunn, Clement Bryce (translator), *Peebles to the Play* (Selkirk, James Lewis, 1904)

Gunn, Clement Bryce, *The Book of the Cross Kirk, Peebles, AD 1261-1560* (Selkirk, James Lewis, 1904)

Gunn, *The Book of the Cross Kirk, Peebles, A.D. 1560-1690, Presbytery and Episcopacy* (Neidpath Press 1912)

Gunn, Clement Bryce, *The Church and Monastery of the Holy Cross of Peebles*, (James Lewis, Selkirk, 1909)

Gunn, Clement Bryce, *The Manual of the Cross Kirk* (Neidpath Press, 1914)

Haddon, A.W. & Stubbs, W. *Councils and ecclesiastical documents relating to Great Britain and Ireland* (Clarendon Press 1869)

Hannah, Ian C., *Screens and Lofts in Scottish Churches* (Proceedings of the Society of Antiquaries of Scotland, Vol 70, 1936)

MacGibbon, D. & Ross, T., *The ecclesiastical architecture of Scotland, Vol 3* (D. Douglas, Edinburgh, 1896)

Renwick, Robert, *Extracts from the Records of the Burgh of Peebles*, (Scottish Burgh Records Society, Glasgow, Vol 1, 1872; Vol II, 1910)

Renwick, Robert, *A Peebles Aisle and Monastery* (Glasgow: Carson & Nicol, 1897)

Renwick, Robert, *Peebles: Burgh and Parish in Early History*, (Peebles, A Redpath, 1903)

Renwick, Robert, *Peebles during the Reign of Queen Mary* (Neidpath Press, 1903)

Renwick, Robert, *The Burgh of Peebles, Glenaings from its Records, 1604-52* (Neidpath Press, 1912)

Royal Commission on the Ancient and Historical Monuments of Scotland (RCAHMS), *An Inventory of the Ancient Monuments of Peeblesshire*, 1967, Vol II

Salway, Peter, *Roman Britain*, (Clarendon Press, 1981)

Steer, K. A., *Two Unrecorded Early Christian Stones* (Proceedings of the Society of Antiquaries of Scotland, Vol 101, 1968-69)

Somerset Fry, Plantagenet & Fiona, *The History of Scotland* (Routledge & Kegan Paul, 1982)

Veitch, Professor John, *The History and Poetry of the Scottish Border* (William Blackwood and Sons, Vol II, Edinburgh, 1878)

Ward, A.W. & A. R. Waller (2000). The Cambridge History of English and American Literature Vol 2. (New York, 2000), quoted at Bartleby.com

Wood, Marguerite, editor, *The Balcarres Papers and the Foreign Correspondence of Marie de Lorrain* (Scottish History Society, 1923)

www.canmore.org.uk/site/51521/peebles-cross-kirk

www.en.wikipedia.org/wiki/Saint_Nicholas

FURTHER READING

Ireland, Ronald, *The Bloody Covenant, Crown and Kirk in Conflict*, (The History Press, 2010)

Illustrations - Sources and Credits

Cover, pages 1 (Cross Kirk), 20, 23, 32 ("new" doorway), 36, 40, 41, 46, 48, Inside back cover, Back Cover: © Steve Dubé

Inside Front Cover, pages 10, 32 (excavated cist), 33 © Historic Environment Scotland (HES)

Title page: Anon

Pages 1, (statue of Alexander III, St Giles, Edinburgh), 3: www.en.wikipedia.org

Page 4: © Parker Library, Corpus Christi College, Cambridge www.theparkerlibrary.wordpress.com/2015/07

Page 7: www.alchetron.com

Page 8: www.forbes.com

Page 9: www.learn.columbia.edu/treasuresofheaven/saints/Nicholas

Pages 16 and 35: Gunn, Clement Bryce, The Church and Monastery of the Holy Cross of Peebles, 1909.

Page 21: http//commons.wikimedia.org/wiki/File:John_Knox

Page 26-27: Map by Aled A. Thomson, The Burgh of Peebles, Gleanings from its Records by Robert Renwick

Page 30 and 45 © National Library of Scotland www .nls.uk/hutton-drawings, Creative Commons licence, all rights reserved

Page 52: Emma Scott

Seal of Cross Kirk
"Abbot" John Turnbull,
undated